This journal belongs to:

....

A child will be born to us.

God will give a son to us.

He will be responsible for leading the people.

His name will be Wonderful Counselor,

Powerful God, Father Who Lives Forever,

Prince of Peace.

Isaiah 9:6

And God's peace will keep your hearts and minds in Christ Jesus. The peace that God gives is so great that we cannot understand it.

Philippians 4:7

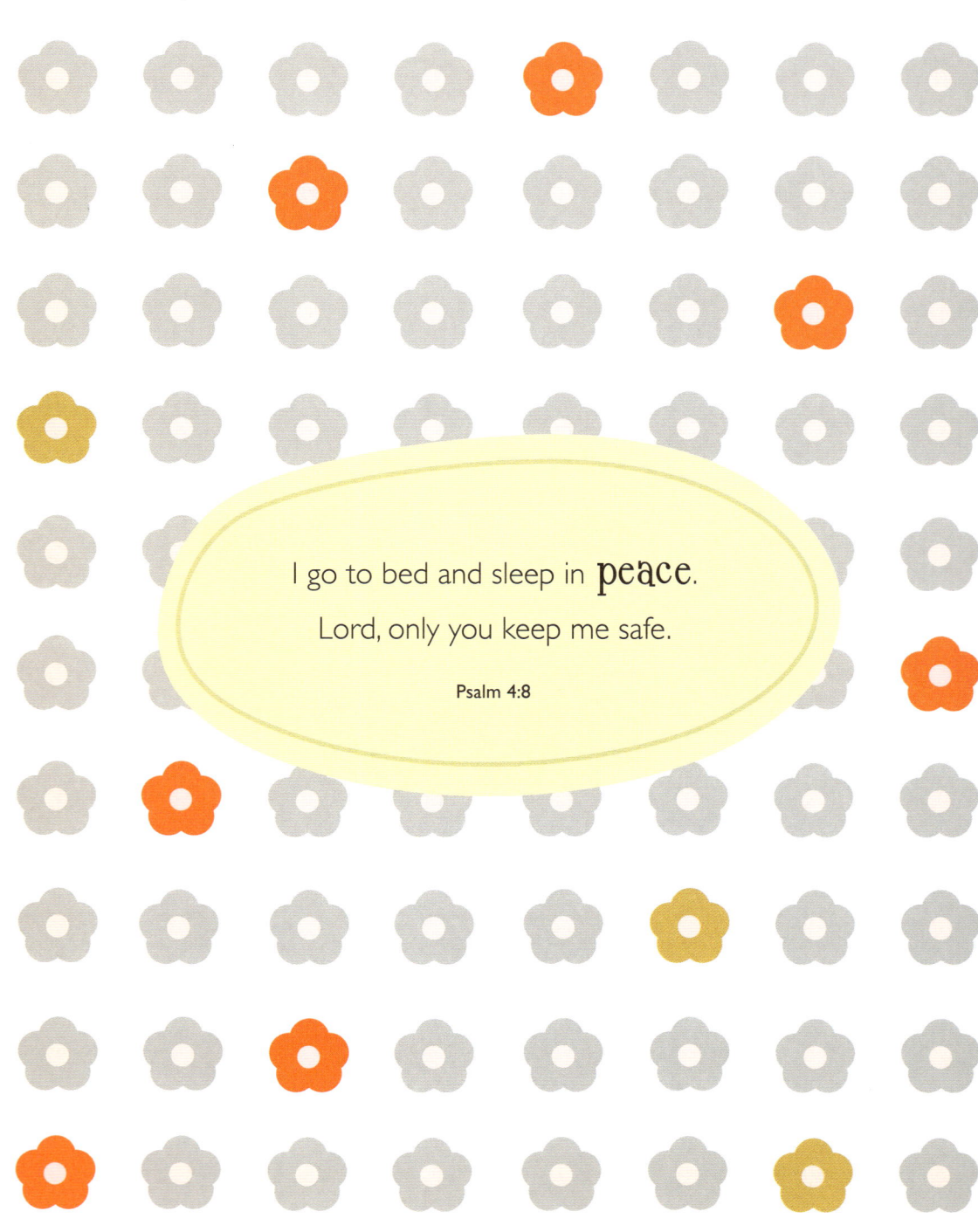

May the Lord bless you and keep you.
May the Lord show you his kindness.
May he have mercy on you.
May the Lord watch over you
and give you peace.

Numbers 6:24–26

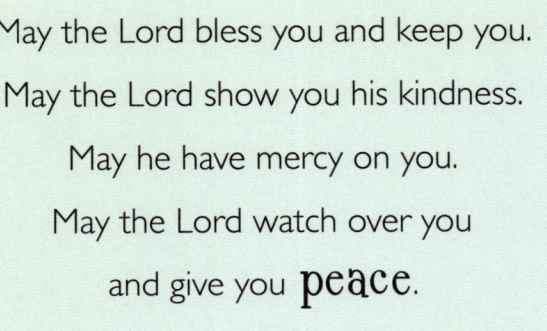

I leave you **peace**. My peace I give you.
I do not give it to you as the world does.
So don't let your hearts be troubled.
Don't be afraid.

John 14:27

Lord, all our success

is because of what you have done.

So give us peace.

Isaiah 26:12

Now, brothers, I say good-bye.
Live in harmony. Do what I have asked you to do.
Agree with each other, and live in peace.
Then the God of love and peace will be with you.

2 Corinthians 13:11

The God who gives **peace**

be with you all. Amen.

Romans 15:33

Wisdom will make your life pleasant.
It will bring you **peace**.

Proverbs 3:17

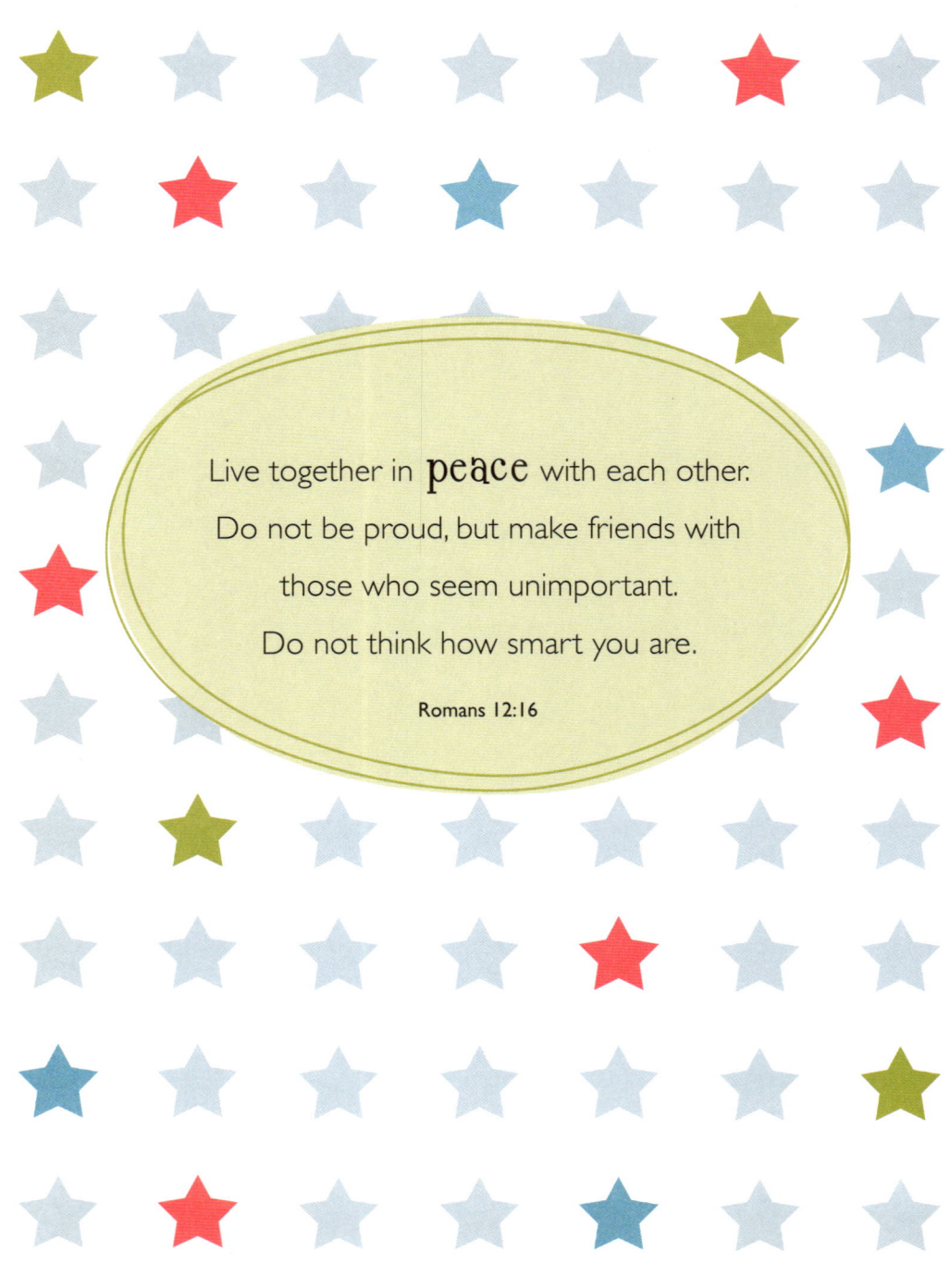

Those who plan evil mean to lie.
But those who plan **peace** will be happy.

Proverbs 12:20

Those who love your teachings
will find true **peace**.
Nothing will defeat them.

Psalm 119:165

How beautiful is the person who comes over the mountains to bring good news. How beautiful is the one who announces peace. He brings good news and announces salvation.

Isaiah 52:7

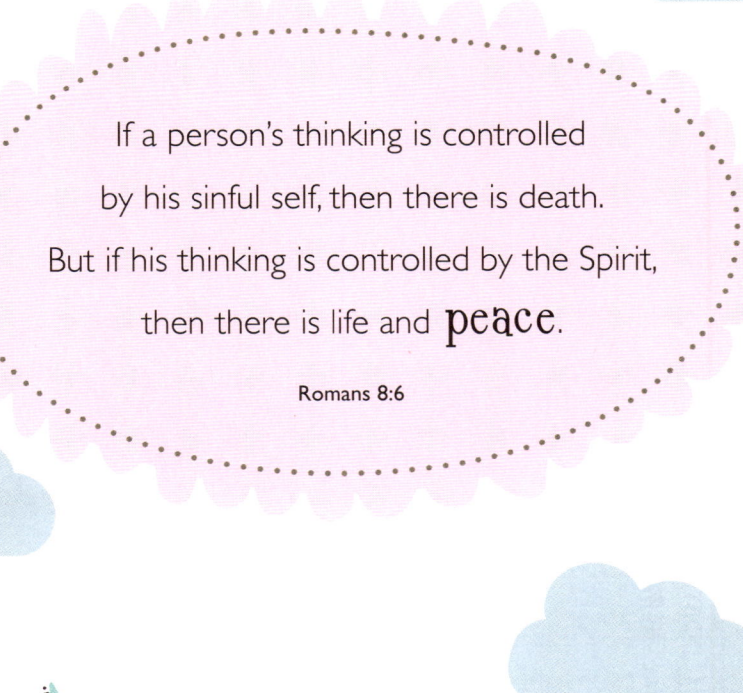

If a person's thinking is controlled by his sinful self, then there is death. But if his thinking is controlled by the Spirit, then there is life and peace.

Romans 8:6

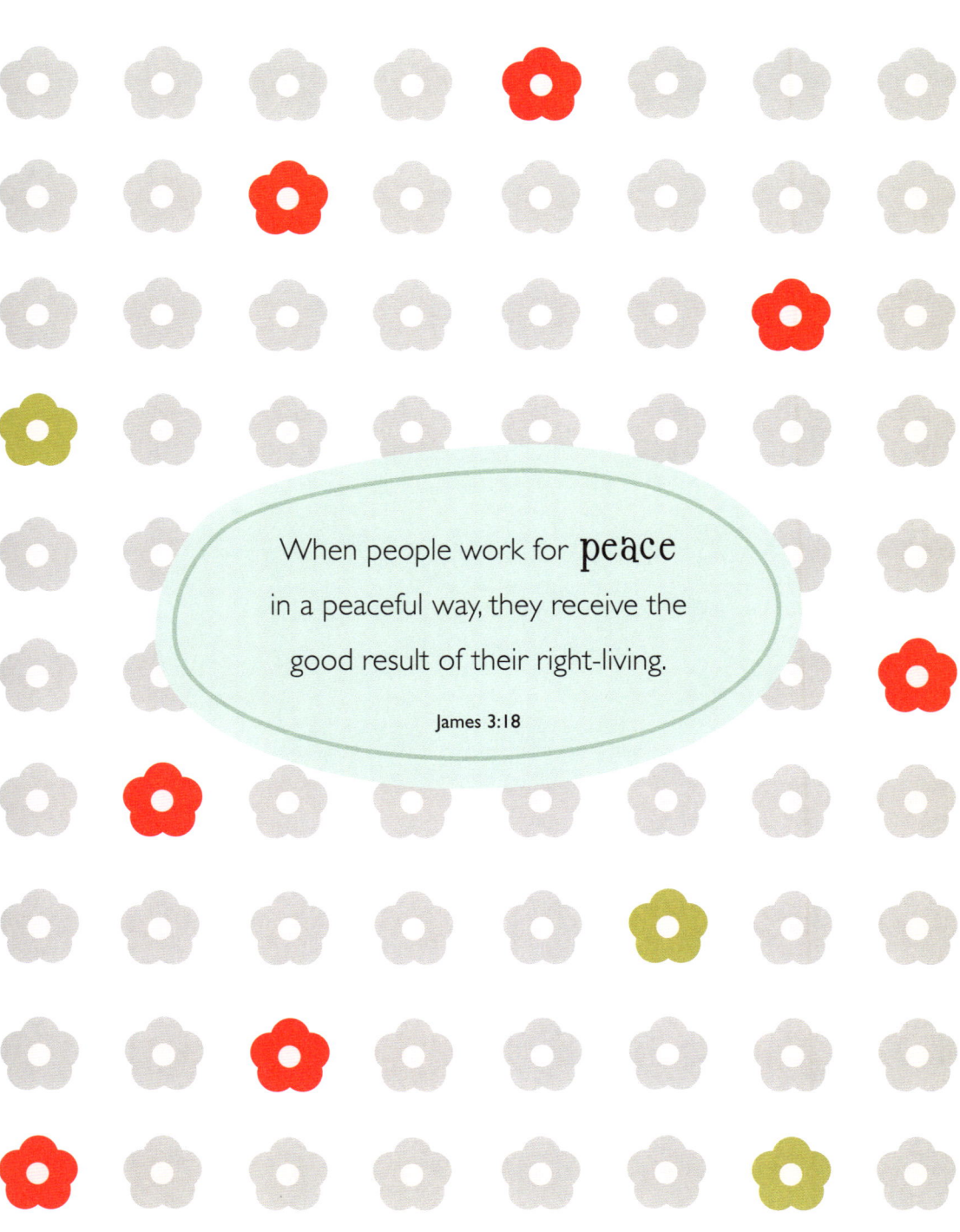

"The mountains may disappear,
and the hills may come to an end.
But my love will never disappear.
My promise of peace will not come to an end,"
says the Lord who shows mercy to you.

Isaiah 54:10

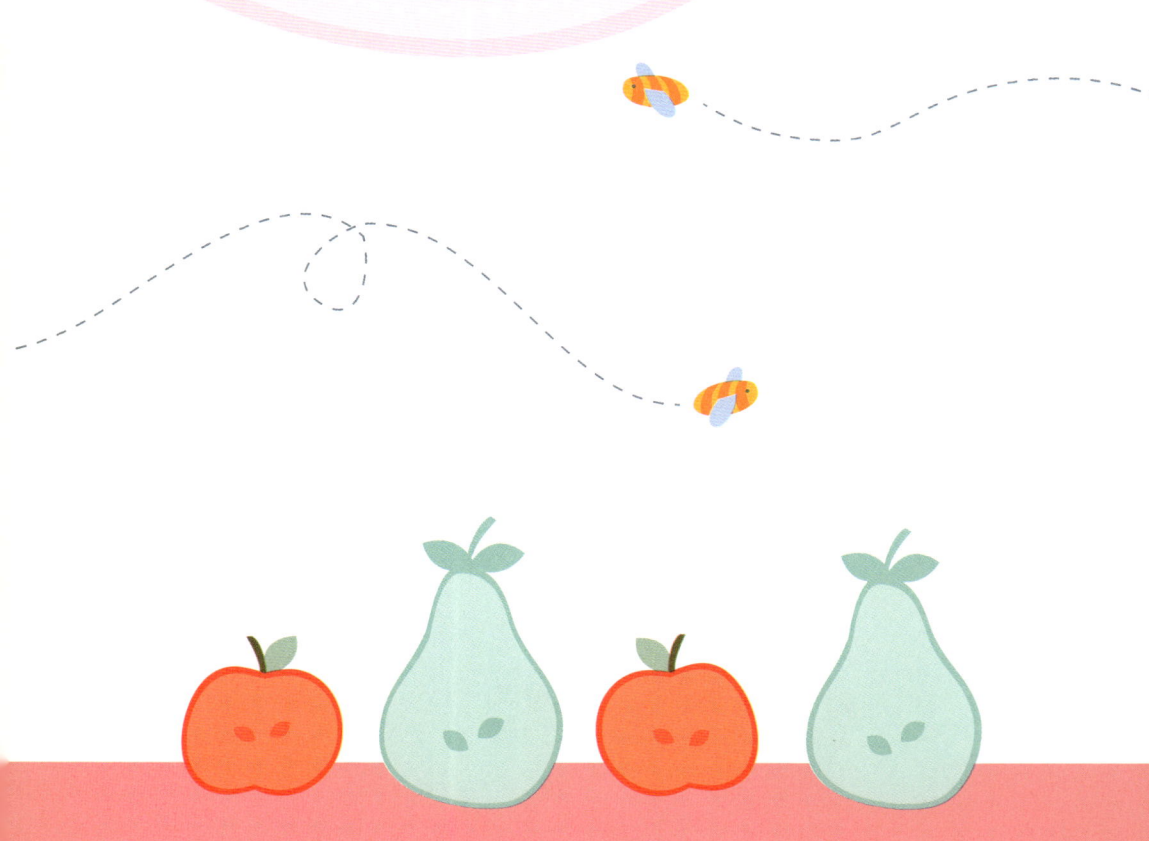

I told you these things so that you can have peace in me. In this world you will have trouble. But be brave! I have defeated the world!

John 16:33

We have been made right with God because of our faith. So we have **peace** with God through our Lord Jesus Christ.

Romans 5:1

You, Lord, give true **peace**.
You give peace to those who depend on you.
You give peace to those who trust you.

Isaiah 26:3

Remind the believers to do these things: to be under the authority of rulers and government leaders, to obey them and be ready to do good, to speak no evil about anyone, to live in peace with all, to be gentle and polite to all people.

Titus 3:1–2

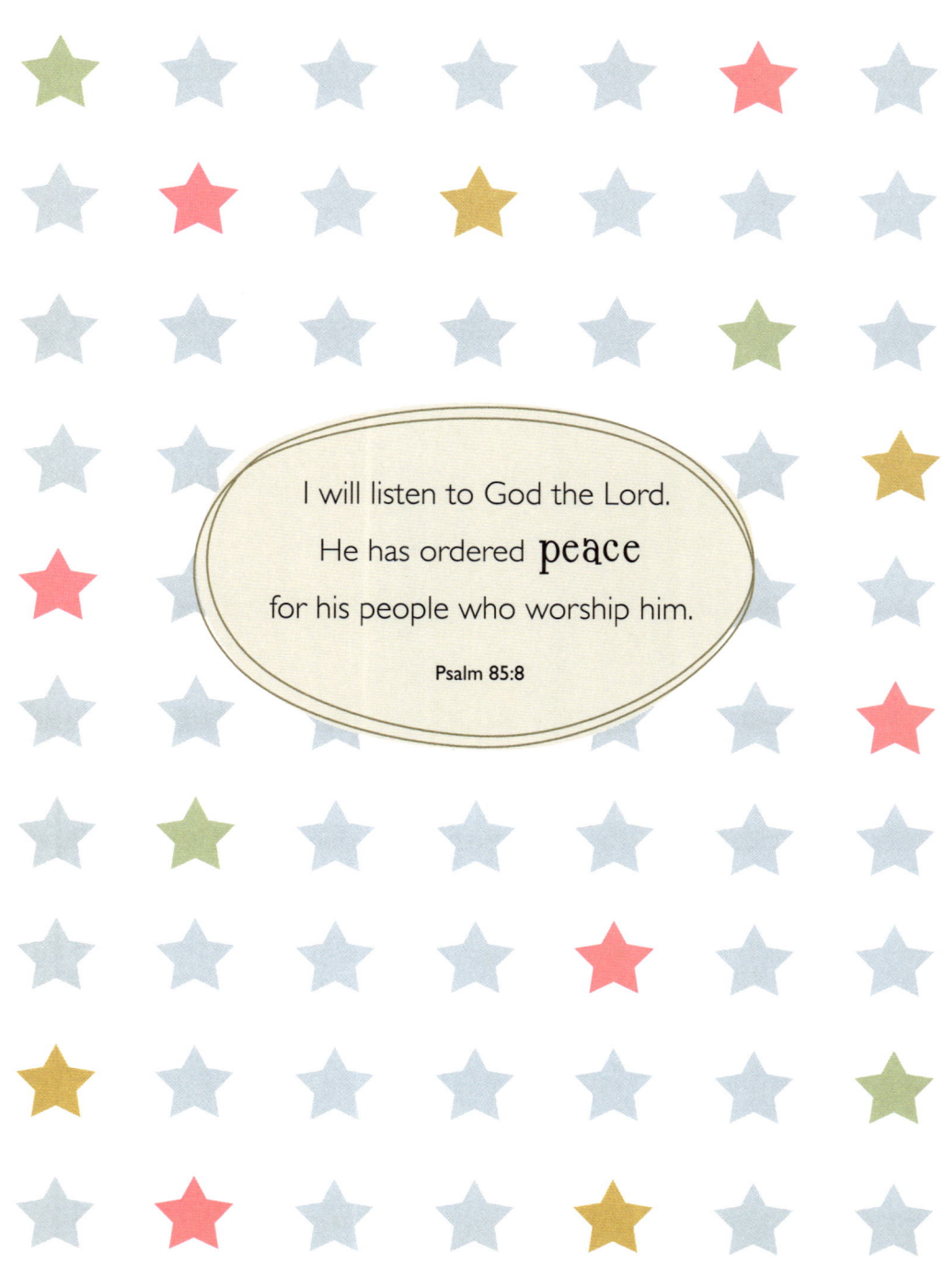

But the wisdom that comes from God is like this: First, it is pure. Then it is also **peaceful**, gentle, and easy to please. This wisdom is always ready to help those who are troubled and to do good for others. This wisdom is always fair and honest.

James 3:17

But the Spirit gives love, joy, peace, patience, kindness, goodness, faithfulness, gentleness, self-control. There is no law that says these things are wrong.

Galatians 5:22–23

So stand strong, with the belt of truth tied around your waist. And on your chest wear the protection of right living. And on your feet wear the Good News of peace to help you stand strong.

Ephesians 6:14–15

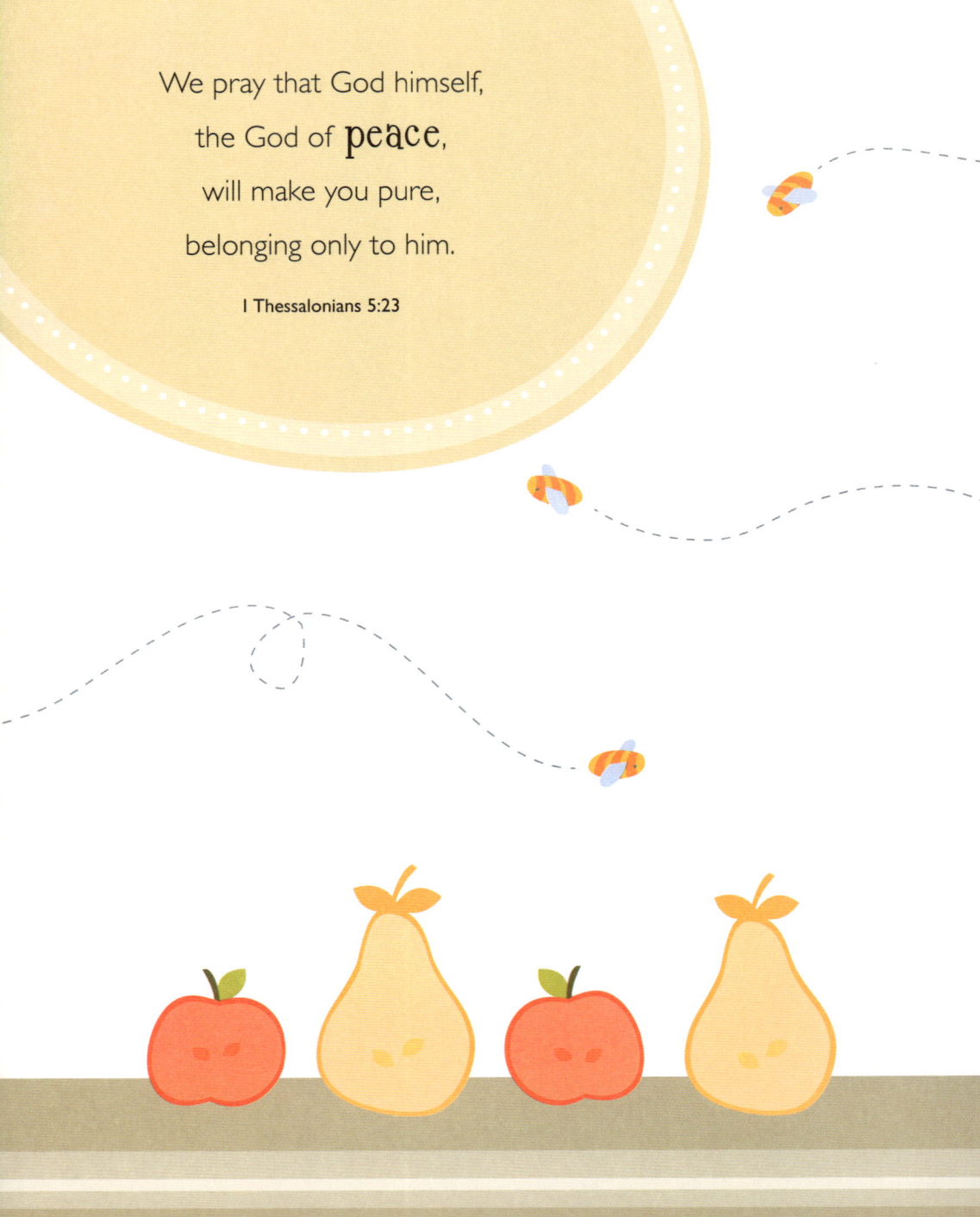

So let us try to do what makes peace and helps one another.

Romans 14:19

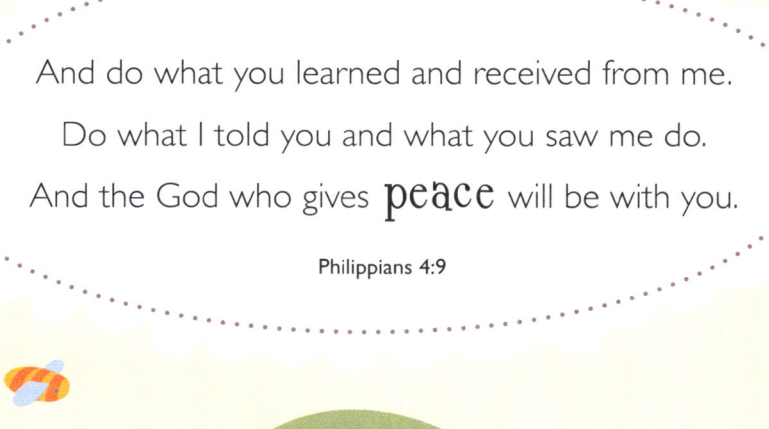

And do what you learned and received from me. Do what I told you and what you saw me do. And the God who gives peace will be with you.

Philippians 4:9

First, I tell you to pray for all people.
Ask God for the things people need, and be thankful to him.
You should pray for kings and for all who have authority.
Pray for the leaders so that we can have
quiet and *peaceful* lives—lives full
of worship and respect for God.

1 Timothy 2:1–2

We do not enjoy punishment.
Being punished is painful at the time.
But later, after we have learned from
being punished, we have peace, because
we start living in the right way.

Hebrews 12:11

Then wolves will live in **peace** with lambs.
And leopards will lie down to rest with goats.
Calves, lions and young bulls will eat together.
And a little child will lead them.

Isaiah 11:6

The God who brings peace will soon defeat Satan and give you power over him. The grace of our Lord Jesus be with you.

Romans 16:20